Garfield

by the
pound

BY: JIM DAVIS

BALLANTINE BOOKS · NEW YORK

Library of Congress Catalog Card Number: 91-92161

ISBN: 0-345-37579-3

Manufactured in the United States of America

First Edition: March 1992

10 9 8 7 6 5 4 3

KNOW YOUR CAT MOODS
HAPPY
SAD
INWARDLY REMORSEFUL, YET CALMLY CONTEMPLATIVE
GURGLE
HUNGRY

GARFIELD
DINGLE
DINGLE DINGLE
© 1990 United Feature Syndicate, Inc.
DINGLE DINGLE DINGL
DINGLE DINGLE DINGLE
DINGLE DINGLE DING
DINGLE DINGLE
DINGLE DING
DINGLE! DINGLE! DINGL
DINGLE DINGLE DINGLE
SMACK!
YOU HAD TO GET HIM A RUBBER DINGLE BALL FOR CHRISTMAS, DIDN'T YOU?!
DINGLE DINGLE
SPLAT!
JIM DAVIS 1-6-91

GARFIELD

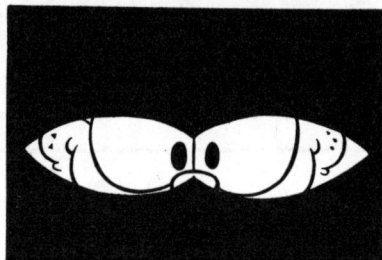

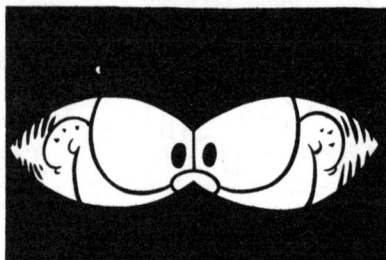

ALL RIGHT!!! ALL RIGHT!!! I'LL FIX BREAKFAST!!!!

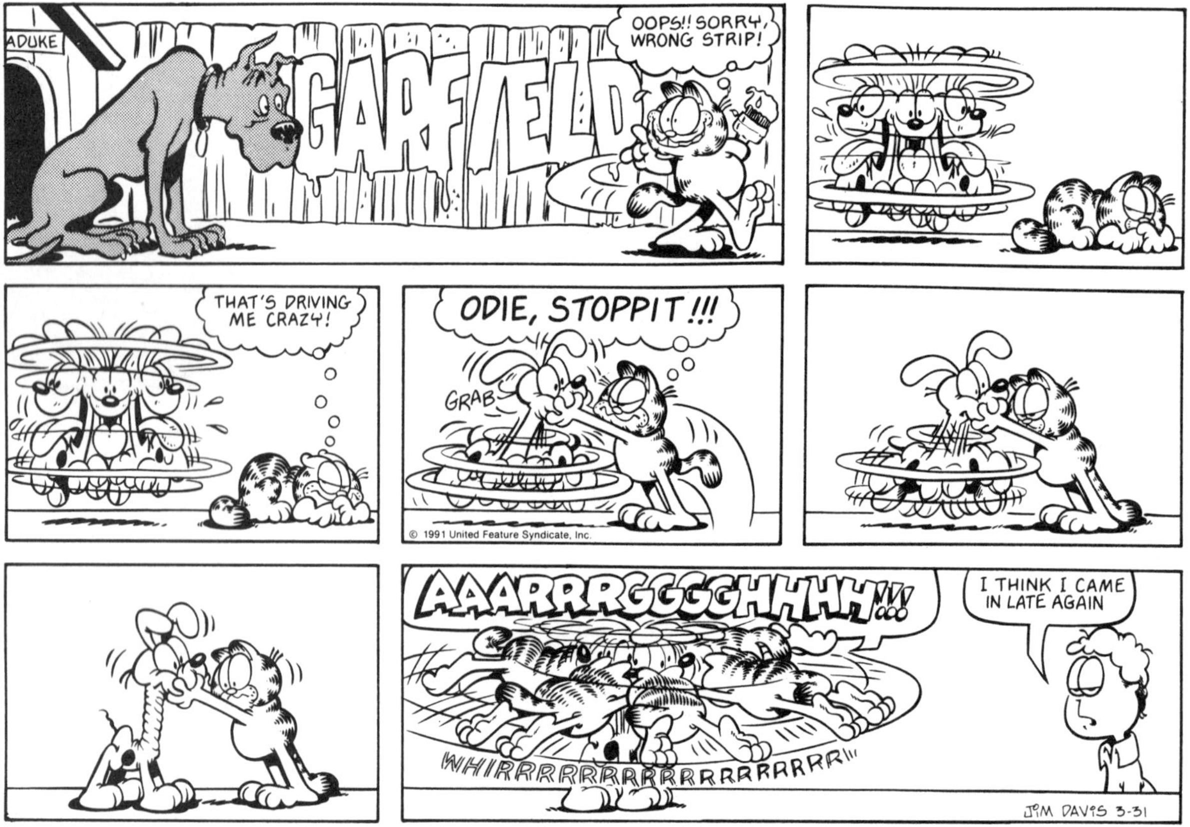

ADUKE
GARFIELD
OOPS!! SORRY, WRONG STRIP!
THAT'S DRIVING ME CRAZY!
ODIE, STOPPIT!!!
GRAB
© 1991 United Feature Syndicate, Inc.
AAARRRGGGGHHHH!!!
WHIRRRRRRRRRRRRRRRRR
I THINK I CAME IN LATE AGAIN
JIM DAVIS 3-31

UH... GARFIELD...

BECAUSE NAP ATTACKS CAN STRIKE ANYTIME, ANYWHERE, WITHOUT WARNING, THAT'S WHY

JIM DAVIS 4-15

JIM DAVIS 4-16

© 1991 United Feature Syndicate, Inc.

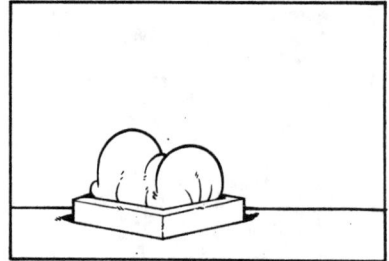

STRIPS, SPECIALS OR BESTSELLING BOOKS...
GARFIELD'S ON EVERYONE'S MENU

Don't miss even one episode in the Tubby Tabby's hilarious series!

BIRTHDAYS, HOLIDAYS, OR ANY DAY...

Keep GARFIELD on your calendar all year 'round!